Department of the Environment

The Right To Buy

A national follow-up survey of tenants of council homes in England

Peter Lynn

London: HMSO

First published 1991
ISBN 0 11 752372 0

CONTENTS

List of Tables

List of Figures

1. INTRODUCTION

1. A major objective of government policy over the last decade has been to extend home ownership to a wider range and greater proportion of the population. The Right to Buy (RTB), introduced as Chapter 1 of the 1980 Housing Act, has been the most significant policy initiative in this context. To aid assessment of the effect and outcome of the policy a national survey of tenants and buyers of council homes was carried out for the Department of the Environment by Social and Community Planning Research (SCPR) in 1985–86 (Kerr, 1988). This survey aimed to identify which factors encourage or discourage take-up of the RTB scheme, to gauge attitudes towards the scheme, and to evaluate the experiences of people who had bought their homes under RTB. In 1989 the Department of the Environment asked SCPR to go back to the sample of addresses that were council tenancies in 1985-86 (but not to those people who had already bought their home) and re-interview the occupants in order to gauge how, if at all, attitudes towards RTB and experiences of it had altered since the earlier survey amongst people who had not bought their homes at that time. This report presents the results of that 1989 follow-up survey comparing them, where appropriate, with the 1985–86 survey findings.

The Contents of this Report

2. At a number of addresses the residents had bought their home from the council since the 1985–86 survey. The characteristics of these 'new buyers' are compared, in Chapter 2, to those people who were still tenants, and to those who had already bought their home at the time of the earlier survey. Chapter 3 discusses the attitudes of tenants towards home ownership and RTB and compares them with those of the new buyers, and Chapter 4 looks at income and housing costs. Chapter 5 discusses maintenance and repairs, and Chapter 6 analyses the new buyers' experiences of the buying process.

3. It should be noted that the percentages given in tables in this report have been rounded up or down to the nearest whole number, and consequently will not always add to 100. Also, the base presented for a particular subgroup may vary slightly from table to table as respondents who have not aswered the question, or not given sufficient information, have usually been excluded.

Survey Method

4. Interviewing was carried out in May 1989. A copy of the explanatory letter which the interviewer left with all contacted sample members is included as Appendix A. The questionnaire used was essentially a repeat of that used for the 1985–86 survey, in order to allow direct comparison of results. A few necessary adaptations were made to take account of changes over time and some new questions added. A copy of the questionnaire is included in a full methodological report of the survey (Lynn, 1990) available direct from SCPR at 35 Northampton Square, London EC1V 0AX.

5. A full description of the method used to sample addresses for the 1985–86 survey appears in Prescott-Clarke and Morrissey, 1988, and is summarised in Kerr, 1988. Addresses were selected with equal probabilities, and the sample was representative of all properties rented from LAs in England. All the tenants' addresses issued in 1985–86 were re-issued for the current study

(including those where no interview was obtained in 1985–86) except for a very small number where the property was found (in the earlier survey) not to be eligible for purchase under RTB.

6. The number of addresses issued to interviewers was 1240. After excluding 54 addresses that proved to be "deadwood" (eg vacant properties) the overall response rate achieved was 78%. It was 80% at addresses that had produced a productive interview on the 1985–86 survey, and 66% at other addresses. The number of interviews completed was 920. A detailed description of the response appears in the methodological report.

7. Where possible the person interviewed was the same person who had responded to the 1985-86 survey or, if they were unavailable, their spouse or partner. Where the previous respondent was no longer resident at the address the current tenant was interviewed or, if they were unavailable, their spouse or partner. Thus, in all cases the interview was carried out either with the householder in whose name the property was rented or their spouse or partner. Two thirds of the achieved interviews were with either the same person who had been interviewed in 1985-86 or their spouse or partner. A full description of who was interviewed appears in the methodological report.

Key Findings

8. Of the addresses that had been council tenancies at the time of the 1985-86 survey, 10% had since been bought under RTB, and were thus now owner-occupied. These 'new buyer households' exhibited characteristics that were broadly similar to, although slightly less pronounced than, those who had bought under RTB prior to the 1985-86 survey: compared with council tenants, new buyer households tended to be larger than average (para. 23), to contain more wage earners than average (para. 117), to have a higher than average income (para. 114), and had bought larger than average properties (para. 19).

9. The new buyers were almost all pleased that they had bought their home, although most had found the buying process difficult (para. 150), and a significant minority had subsequently experienced problems in keeping up payments (para. 159).

10. Nearly all the tenants had heard of RTB, but a large proportion did not know whether they would qualify to buy their home under RTB. 6% were currently in the process of trying to buy their home, and a further 4% had tried in the past but not gone through with the purchase (para. 45).

11. The most common reasons given by tenants for not buying their homes were similar to those given by tenants in the earlier survey: worries about being able to afford the repayments, being unable to get a loan, and being too old to buy, although the proportion perceiving themselves to be too old appeared to have fallen slightly. A sizeable minority said that they had simply never considered the possibility of buying (para. 57).

12. A new question, asking tenants whether certain changes might make them consider buying their home, identified financial considerations as being the most likely to affect future buying decisions: around half of the tenants thought that they would be likely to consider buying their home if there was an improvement in their own financial circumstances, or if they could buy their home without paying out more than they were currently paying in rent. Other hypothetical changes, such as the transfer of their home to a new landlord, or a change in family circumstances, were seen as being less likely to cause them to consider buying (paras. 78-96).

2. Characteristics of Tenants and Buyers

13. 10% of the people interviewed were found to have bought their home subsequent to the 1985-86 survey and were thus now owner-occupiers. This was a larger number than had been anticipated, since national RTB sales between late 1985 and early 1989 were approximately 7% of the council stock at the earlier date. Consequently the questionnaire had been designed so that these 'new buyers' were asked only a very limited range of questions, the intention being to then carry out some small-scale qualitative follow-up work. In the event the surprisingly high number of new buyers identified was enough to allow quantitative measurement, so it was subsequently decided to go back and re-interview these people, administering the full range of questions that buyers had been asked in the 1985-86 survey. These re-interviews were carried out in August and September 1989. This chapter compares the new buyers to tenants in demographic terms and in terms of a very limited range of attitude questions. Comparisons of their attitudes towards RTB and home purchase and their expectations for the future appear in Chapter 3.

14. It was to be expected that these new buyers might have somewhat different characteristics to those who had already bought by 1986. One possible explanation for the fact that they had not bought by 1986 but had by 1989 could have been that they had only become eligible under RTB during the intervening period. However, this was not the explanation as 81% of the new buyers had been living at their current address for at least five years, and only three of them had been there less than two years. Indeed, 78% of them had been interviewed at the address in the 1985-6 survey. More plausibly the new buyers might have been less willing and/or less able to buy than the earlier buyers. This was assessed by comparing some characteristics of the new buyers with pre-1986 buyers to see whether, for example, the new buyers tended to occupy different types of properties, or were more financially disadvantaged.

15. The comparisons presented in the remainder of this chapter should not be interpreted as being conclusive because of the relatively small number of new buyers in the sample (96). Nevertheless, they do suggest that the new buyers were less likely than earlier buyers to have bought a home with 3 or more bedrooms, and less likely to have a garage. New buying households were also, on average, smaller than the earlier buying households. Furthermore, findings reported in Chapter 4 suggest that compared to the earlier buyers, the new buyers were more likely not to have any wage earners in the household. Compared with council tenants, however, on average the new buyers had higher incomes and lived in larger properties.

16. Many of these variables are, of course, correlated with one another, e.g. size of household and size of property, income and size of property, so, subsequent to the presentation of the initial results, the Department commissioned SCPR to carry out a multivariate analysis to examine the *relative* importance of these variables in discriminating between those who had decided to buy their home and those who had not done so. This analysis found that most of the difference between tenants and new buyers could be explained by differences in household income, and in type of property. Once allowance

had been made for these two variables, no significant differences remained between subgroups. (Technical details of the multivariate analysis appear in Appendix B.)

Type of Property

17. New buyers were more likely than tenants to live in more desirable properties. One half of the new buyers lived in semi-detached houses, compared with only a third of tenants. Slightly more new buyers than tenants lived in end- or mid-terrace houses, but none of them lived in bungalows and only 10% lived in flats or maisonettes, compared to 5% of the tenants who lived in bungalows and 36% who lived in flats or maisonettes. These findings are very similar to the comparison of those who had already bought their home in 1986 with those who had not (Kerr, 1988, p.7), although slightly more of the new buyers lived in flats or maisonettes than the pre-1986 buyers, and slightly fewer lived in semi-detached houses.

Table 1: **Property Type**

	Tenants (1989)	New buyers	Pre-1986 buyers
	%	%	%
Semi-detached house	33	52	56
End-terrace house	9	18	15
Mid-terrace house	17	20	24
Bungalow	5	0	1
Flat/Maisonette	36	10	3
Base	824	96	1,031

18. Half of the tenants of houses (51%) lived in semi-detached houses, a quarter (27%) in mid-terrace houses and 1 in 7 (14%) in end-terrace houses. Others lived in semi-detached bungalows (6%), detached bungalows (1%), and detached houses (1%). The vast majority of tenants of flats (87%) were tenants of purpose-built flats, 11% lived in purpose-built maisonettes, and 2% in converted flats.

Size of Property

19. The findings suggest that, among new buyers, the trend was towards purchasing smaller properties than those who had already bought in 1986. 3% of the new buyers had bought 1-bedroom and 27% 2-bedroom properties, compared with 0% and 20% respectively of those who bought prior to 1986. Conversely, only 70% had purchased homes with 3 or more bedrooms, compared with 80% in 1986.

20. Among tenants, those living in houses had more bedrooms than those living in flats, two-thirds of them having three or more, compared with only 1 in 10 of the tenants of flats.

Table 2: **Number of Bedrooms**

	Tenants (1989)	
	Houses	Flats
	%	%
One	5	40
Two	30	50
Three	61	10
Four or more	4	0
Base	534	290

21. Three-quarters of tenants thought that their home had about the right number of rooms (78% of tenants of houses and 75% of tenants of flats), but a very significant minority thought they had too few rooms (15% of tenants of houses and 22% of tenants of flats).

Facilities

22. New buyers of houses were only slightly more likely to have a private garden both front and back (92%) than tenants of houses (86%). They were almost twice as likely to have their own garage (22%) as tenants of houses (12%), but this figure was lower than that for pre-1986 buyers (28%).

Household Type

23. New buying households tended to be larger than tenant households, but not as large as households who had bought prior to 1986. In 1989, 33% of new buying households were 'large adult households' with three or more adults (GHS definition—see OPCS, 1989, p212), compared with only 12% of tenant households, but 40% of those who had bought prior to 1986. Conversely, 11% of new buying households consisted of a single person, compared with 31% of tenant households, but only 5% of those who had bought prior to 1986. This increase in the number of buying households that consisted of a single person was due almost entirely to an increase in purchases by single pensioners: 9% of new buyers were single pensioners, compared with only 3% of pre-1986 buyers.

Table 3: **Household type**

	Tenants (1989)	New buyers	Pre-1986 buyers
	%	%	%
One adult	31	11	5
Two adults	27	26	27
Small family	19	17	16
Large family	10	13	12
Large adult household	12	33	40
Base	824	96	1,031

Activity Status and Marital Status

24. Heads of new buying households were much more likely to be in paid employment than their tenant counterparts. Two-thirds of the new buying households were headed by someone in full-time employment, compared with only a quarter of tenant households. These proportions were very similar to those observed for buyers and tenants respectively in 1986. A third of heads of tenant households were fully retired, compared to only one in six of heads of new buying households. (Results of the 1988 LFS showed a similar pattern, with over 40% of tenant household heads over retirement age, compared to only 20% of RTB purchasers.)

Table 4: **Head of Household's Activity Status**

	Tenants	New buyers
	%	%
Full-time employment	27	66
Part-time employment	5	5
Unemployed, looking for work	9	2
Long-term sick	7	0
Wholly retired	32	17
Keeping house	16	8
Other	1	1
Base	819	95

25. Buyers were more likely than tenants to be living with a partner. Nearly 8 out of 10 of the new buyers were married or living as married with their partner, compared with less than half of the tenants. The remainder of the tenants were single, widowed, divorced or separated. (These figures are based on the status of the respondent rather than the head of household. 87% of respondents were the head of household, and 12% were the spouse/partner of the head of household).

Table 5: **Respondent's Marital Status**

	Tenants	New buyers
	%	%
Married/living with partner	48	78
Single	14	4
Widowed	22	13
Divorced or separated	16	5
Base	824	96

Location

26. There were no obvious differences between new buyers and tenants in either the size of the town in which they lived, or the type of area in which it was situated (inner city/other urban/suburban/suburban fringe/rural). A pattern had been found in 1985-86, when sales were less common in large cities and conurbations (Kerr 1988, para. 43). The failure of the current survey to identify a pattern could partly be due to the relatively small numbers of new buyers, so interpretation is difficult.

27. Slightly more new buyers (52%) than tenants (46%) lived in the south of England[1]. The two standard regions that contained particularly few new buyers were the north and north-west, which together accounted for 19% of tenants but only 7% of new buyers.

The Area, and Attitudes Towards it

28. On average, new buyers lived in more attractive areas than tenants, in terms of size and composition of estates.

29. Equal proportions of tenants and of new buyers considered their home to be part of an estate (78%), but of those the new buyers tended to live on smaller estates than the tenants. 1 in 3 of the new buyers living on estates thought that the estate contained no more than 100 homes, whereas fewer than 1 in 6 of the tenants said they lived on such small estates.

[1]The south is defined as the following four standard regions: Greater London, South East, South West, and East Anglia.

30. 80% of the new buyers considered that they lived in an area which was all or mostly houses, compared with 63% of tenants. Of the tenants, 13% considered themselves to be living in an area of all or mostly flats, whereas only one of the new buyers thought that.

31. Not surprisingly, the majority of council tenants (72%) lived on an estate or street that was surrounded by an area of mostly council housing. 22% were in an area of mixed council and private housing, and only 5% were in an area of mostly private housing.

32. All respondents were asked to classify their estate (or street, in the case of those not living on an estate) as a very good place to live, a fairly good place to live, not a very good place to live, or not at all a good place to live. The new buyers gave slightly more favourable responses than the tenants, but the differences were small. Slightly more new buyers than tenants thought that their estate was a very good place to live, and slightly fewer new buyers than tenants classified their estate as not a very good or not at all a good place to live. These views of new buyers were very similar to those given in 1986 by pre-1986 buyers, and the views of tenants in 1989 are very similar to those of tenants in 1986. The survey provided no evidence that council estates were becoming better or worse places to live.

Table 6: **Perceptions of the Area as a Place to Live**

	Tenants	New buyers
	%	%
A very good place to live	32	39
A fairly good place to live	53	53
Not a very good place to live	10	5
Not at all a good place to live	4	3
Base	824	96

33. Nine out of ten of the new buyers thought that their estate was either a very popular or a fairly popular place to live, as did nearly eight out of ten of the tenants, but one in five of the new buyers expected things on the estate to get worse over the next few years. Slightly fewer of the tenants expected things to get worse. Only one in ten of the new buyers were either dissatisfied or very dissatisfied with the general look of the estate, as were one in five of the tenants, although when asked how well the local authority look after the estate a third of both the new buyers and the tenants replied either 'not very well' or 'not at all well.'

Table 7: **Satisfaction with General Look of Estate**

	Tenants	New buyers
	%	%
Very satisfied	18	15
Satisfied	48	58
Neither satisfied nor dissatisfied	15	15
Dissatisfied	14	11
Very dissatisfied	5	1
Base	822	96

Table 8: **Perceptions of how well Local Authority look after Estate**

	Tenants	New buyers
	%	%
Very well	18	8
Fairly well	52	59
Not very well	22	26
Not at all well	9	6
Base	811	96

34. Six out of ten of the new buyers liked their own house or flat 'very much', compared to just under half of the tenants. In both cases these proportions were a slight increase over those for buyers and tenants respectively in 1986. Indeed, even if we look at the subset of 500 tenants who were respondents in both 1986 and 1989, the proportion liking their home 'very much' rose slightly from 45% to 49%. This effect could be due to, for example, improvements or modernisation having taken place in the interim, but the current analysis cannot confirm this. Of the new buyers, 75 had responded (as tenants) to the 1986 survey. At that stage, 34 liked their home 'very much', 28 'quite a lot', and 13 'not very much'. In 1989 44 liked their home 'very much', 29 'quite a lot', 1 'not very much', and 1 'not at all'.

35. Fewer of the new buyers (14%) than of the tenants (24%) thought that their home had been fully modernised by the council within the last ten years. This may be partly explained by the fact that the council would no longer be responsible for the homes of the new buyers, but this alone could not cause such a large effect. It seems likely that councils have been targetting improvements on their worst stock, which was least likely to be purchased under RTB, and this could account for the differences.

Acquaintance with Homeowners

36. The report on the 1986 survey expressed surprise that buyers were no more likely than tenants to have grown up in owner-occupied accommodation (i.e. their parents having been homeowners). The new buyers in 1989 were also no more likely than tenants to have had parents who owned their home, about a third of both groups having had owner-occupying parents. Indeed (as with the buyers in 1986) the new buyers were slightly more likely than tenants to have been the children of council tenants.

37. Current acquaintance with homeowners was much more common amongst the new buyers than amongst the tenants. New buyers were twice as likely as tenants to say that all or most of their family and friends owned their home, three-quarters of them having said that. The proportions saying in 1986 that all or most of their family and friends owned their home were 37% of tenants and 65% of buyers, so in both cases the proportion had risen since 1986. Thus, both homeownership and awareness of it had increased between 1986 and 1989, and this was confirmed by the finding that nearly 4 out of 10 of the tenants and 5 out of 10 of the new buyers said that more of their family and friends owned their home in 1989 than had done so three years earlier. New buyers were also much more likely than tenants to know other people who had bought their council home; 6 out of 10 new buyers, but only 1 in 3 tenants knew five or more such people. Similar numbers of both new buyers and tenants (around 6 out of 10) said in 1989 that they currently knew more people who had bought their council home than they had known three years ago.

38. Reviewing similar findings in 1985-86, Kerr argued that there was evidence of a 'band wagon' effect on sales (Kerr, 1988, para. 77). However, it cannot necessarily be concluded that knowing other homeowners helped encourage people to buy: buyers may well be likely to live in areas where substantial numbers have bought, and would thus be likely to know more homeowners, simply because more of their neighbours were owners. Indeed, the survey showed that the new owners were much more likely than tenants to live in a street or block where a significant proportion of the residents had bought their council homes. Half of the new buyers said that at least half of the people in the street/block had bought their council home, whereas less than 1 in 5 of the tenants said this. (It seems likely that this was because most council housing was developed in relatively homogenous streets/blocks in terms of property type. Consequently, either all the properties in the street/block are of a type likely to sell, or all are of a type unlikely to sell.) The new buyers also appeared to have greater knowledge than the tenants of whether other people in the street/block had bought their home as over 90% of the new buyers knew how many people had bought, compared with only three quarters of the tenants. However, new buyers were more likely to live on smaller estates, so they might be expected to have a better knowledge of the level of sales.

Table 9: **How many people in street/block have bought council home**

	Tenants	New buyers
	%	%
All of them	—	3
Most of them	7	24
About half of them	9	22
A few of them	31	36
One of them	8	1
None of them	23	4
Don't know	23	9
Base	824	96

39. Of those who said that 'a few' or more people in the street/block had bought their council home, 6 out of 10 tenants, and 7 out of 10 of the new buyers said that the number who had bought had increased since 1986.

3. Tenants' and Buyers' Attitudes Towards Homeownership

40. The 1986 survey found that the majority of tenants would ideally prefer to be homeowners. Their main reasons for not purchasing their council home were that they thought they were too old, or could not afford to buy, or because they were dissatisfied with either the property or the area. But there was also a significant minority of tenants who could not recall having heard about the Right to Buy, and many others were not sure if they were eligible. Thus, one of the major aims of the 1989 survey was to investigate whether there had been any change in the reasons why tenants had not bought their home, and whether there had been any increase in knowledge of RTB.

41. There did seem to have been slight increases both in the proportion who had heard of RTB and in the proportion who knew whether or not they were eligible, but substantial numbers (over 40%) still did not know whether they were eligible. The only change in the reasons why tenants had not bought their homes was a slight drop in the proportion perceiving themselves to be too old to buy.

Knowledge of the Right to Buy

42. Overall, 95% of tenants had heard of the Right to Buy. This familiarity was higher amongst tenants of houses (97%) than amongst tenants of flats (92%). In 1986 91% of all tenants had heard of the Right to Buy—93% of tenants of houses and 87% of tenants of flats—so the overall level had increased slightly by 1989[2].

43. Surprisingly, of the tenants who had only heard of RTB since the 1986 survey, only a very small number claimed that they had first heard of the scheme through taking part in the earlier survey. Amongst those who had responded to both surveys there was a slight increase in the numbers saying that they had first heard of RTB through a government leaflet, or that they could not remember how they had first heard of it. However, there was also a slight decrease in the numbers claiming to have first heard of RTB through a council leaflet or from friends or relatives. These discrepancies are undoubtedly at least partly due to memory effects, as respondents were now being asked to remember back over a longer time period.

44. Overall, nearly a third of tenants said they had first heard of RTB through a council leaflet, and a similar number through the TV or press. Tenants in flats were more likely than tenants in houses to claim to have first heard of RTB through friends or relatives, and less likely to have heard of it through leaflets or the TV or press. The new buyers were even more likely than tenants in flats to say they had heard of RTB through friends or relatives. No respondents said they had first heard of RTB through seeing the 'Right to Buy' video (though this does not mean that none had seen the video).

[2] If the new buyers are included in the base, then 96% of households that were tenants in 1986 had heard of RTB by 1989. Furthermore, within the subset of respondents who took part as tenants in both surveys, knowledge of RTB had increased from 93% to 96%. These people were themselves not representative of all tenants, but the fact that knowledge of RTB had increased among them suggests that information about RTB had been successfully disseminated between 1986 and 1989, rather than the increase in knowledge being due to, say, more knowledgeable people having moved in to the sample.

Table 10: **How First Heard of 'Right to Buy'**

	All	Tenants Houses	Flats	New Buyers All
First heard from:	%	%	%	%
Government leaflet	7	8	4	7
Council leaflet	32	34	28	18
TV/press	30	32	27	32
Friends, relatives, neighbours	17	14	23	35
Last survey	–	1	–	2
Other/can't remember	9	8	9	5
Have not heard of RTB	5	3	8	0
Base	824	534	290	82

Eligibility

45. 6% of tenants were currently trying to buy their home and had completed and returned the form RTB1 which initiates the purchase process. A further 4% had tried in the past to buy their home, having returned the RTB1, but did not go through with the purchase. Thus, overall 10% of tenants had at some stage applied to buy their council home. Of these, two-thirds knew what percentage discount they were entitled to, about 1 in 6 could not remember it, and about 1 in 6 said they had not been informed of it. Obviously all new buyers had, by definition, applied to buy their home, so overall 18% of those who had been tenants in 1986 had at some stage applied.

46. Of respondents not currently in the process of trying to buy their home (including those who had applied in the past but not gone through with the purchase) over 4 out of 10 (43%)[3] did not know whether they would qualify to buy their home under RTB. This is only marginally less than the proportion who did not know in 1986 whether they would qualify (47%). A further 4 out of 10 knew that they would qualify, and the rest said they knew that they would not qualify.

47. Ignorance of whether they qualified varied by subgroups (see fig. 1): over half of the tenants of flats did not know, compared with less than 4 out of 10 of the tenants of houses; the proportion not knowing was higher among people living alone than among households containing at least one child under 16, and lowest among other (all-adult) households; slightly more households with a head of household aged under 35 did not know, compared to others; more households headed by a female than those headed by a male did not know; the proportion not knowing was higher than average among households with a low gross weekly income; it was lower than average among households where the head's socio-economic group was non-manual or skilled manual; it was lower among those who had been council tenants at least 5 years, than amongst others.

[3]However, if the new buyers are added in to the base (as they must all have known they were eligible) the proportion not knowing whether they qualified drops to 39%.

Figure 1 **Lack of knowledge of eligibility for RTB**

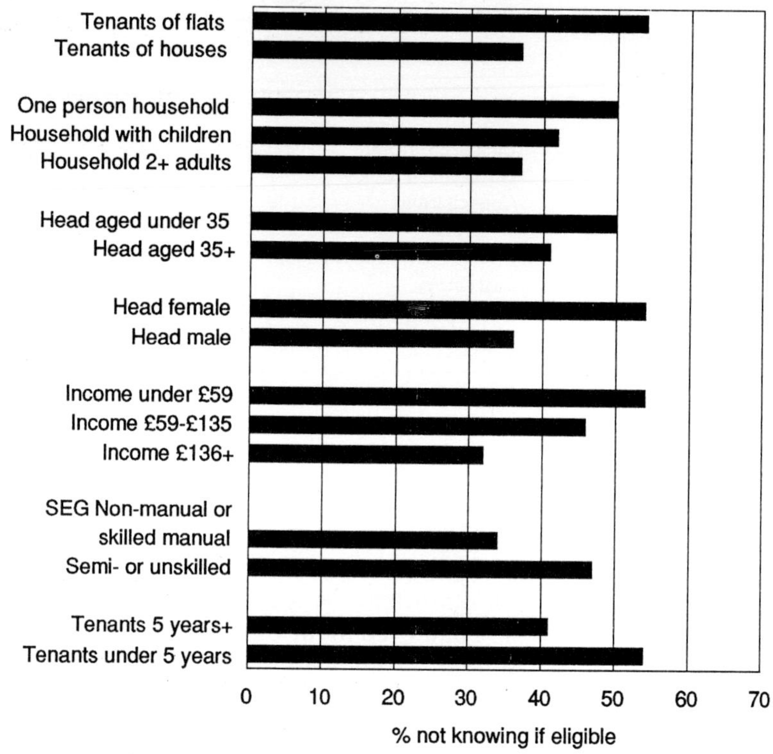

Base: all tenants not currently in process of trying to buy (n=772)

48. Of those who knew that they would qualify, less than 4 out of 10 knew what discount they were entitled to. Again this knowledge was more widespread amongst tenants of houses than amongst tenants of flats.

Table 11: **Knowledge of 'Right to Buy' Entitlement**

	All	Tenants Houses	Flats
	%	%	%
Know would qualify—	40	47	27
discount known	*16*	*20*	*7*
discount not known	*25*	*27*	*21*
Know would not qualify	16	15	17
Don't know if would qualify	43	37	54
Not answered	1	—	2
Base = tenants not currently in process of buying	772	500	272

49. The 1986 survey showed that knowledge of eligibility under RTB was lowest amongst single person households and highest amongst large adult households, and that it was lower when the head of household was in either the youngest or oldest age groups, or the lower socio-economic groups. The relationships between knowledge of eligibility and household type and socio-economic group, seem not to have altered significantly since 1986, but there does appear to have been a change in the effect of the age of the head of household on knowledge of eligibility. In 1989 the youngest and oldest groups both seemed more likely to believe that they were eligible than they did in 1986, while there had been no increase in the level of belief amongst the intermediate

age groups. Consequently, although the youngest and oldest age groups still had lower percentages believing themselves eligible for RTB, the differences with the intermediate groups were no longer great.

Table 12: **Proportion Believing Themselves Eligible for Right to Buy**

Age of head of household	Tenants—1986		Tenants—1989	
	%	(base)	%	(base)
16-34	21	(201)	31	(175)
35-44	48	(120)	42	(108)
45-54	56	(115)	51	(73)
55-64	46	(201)	43	(133)
65-74	46	(193)	43	(168)
75+	22	(116)	39	(111)
All ages	39	(953)	41	(768)

The Buying Process

50. This section is concerned with the 52 tenants (6% of the sample) who in 1989 were in the process of trying to buy their home, and the 34 (4%) who had tried in the past but not gone through with the purchase. Their progress towards completing the purchase is described, including for the latter group, at what point the attempt to buy was abandoned.

51. Of those currently in the process of trying to buy (34 tenants of houses and 18 tenants of flats), one respondent had completed and returned his RTB1, initiating the purchase process, in 1987, 10 had done so in the first half of 1988, 22 in the latter half of 1988, and 19 in the first five months of 1989. Thus, the average 'waiting time' so far was around seven months. Of these 52 respondents, 23 of them remembered being told by the council the full price of their home before discount, 21 remembered being told the discounted price, and 22 said that the council had made a formal offer to sell.

52. Amongst those currently trying to buy there was a high level of optimism about the likelihood that they would complete the purchase: 35 of the 52 thought that it was 'very likely', and a further 13 thought it 'fairly likely', i.e. 9 out of 10 expected to become home owners.

53. Of the 34 respondents who had applied in the past to buy their home but not gone through with the purchase, 6 had applied between 1980 and 1983, 6 in 1984-85, 7 in 1986-87, 8 in 1988 and 3 in 1989. 31 were tenants of houses, and only 3 tenants of flats. 26 remembered having been told the full price of their home by the council, 29 remembered being told the discounted price, and 23 said they had been made a formal offer to sell. Thus, in most cases it seems that the reason for the purchase not being completed was not an unwillingness or inability on the part of the council to make a formal offer to sell. These 34 respondents were asked whether they did not go through with buying because they really only applied to find out the value of their home, or for some other reason; only one said that they had only wanted a valuation, the other 33 had not gone through with the purchase for some other reason.

Tenure Preference

54. Overall, 28% of respondents said that taking everything into account, and assuming they lived in their ideal type of home, they would prefer to rent rather than own their home. 30% of tenants said this, as, somewhat surprisingly, did 4% of new buyers. People living on their own were more likely than others to prefer to rent, as were older respondents. When those two characteristics were combined the proportion preferring to rent rose considerably: half (51%) of

respondents aged 60 or more and living on their own preferred to rent. Not surprisingly, respondents in households with a low gross weekly income were much more likely than others to prefer to rent; nearly half (45%) of those with a gross weekly household income of no more than £58 preferred to rent, while the proportion dropped to just 6% when gross weekly household income rose above £231. The proportion preferring to rent also increased sharply with the age of the head of household, ranging from 11% of those under 35 to 54% of those aged 75 or over. Preference to rent also increased with the length of time that the respondent and/or spouse had been public sector tenants: amongst those who had been tenants for less than five years only 15% preferred to rent, while the proportion rose to 38% of those who had been tenants for twenty years or more.

55. These factors identified as affecting tenure preference were broadly the same as in the 1986 survey, with one exception. The exception was the effect of the age of head of household; in 1986 it was reported that although preference to rent increased with age there was an exception in that the youngest age group contained substantial numbers who would prefer to rent—22% of those with a household head under 25 would have opted to rent compared to only 10% of those aged 25–44. In the 1989 survey the figure for those aged 25–44 had altered little, at 11%, but only 5% of those with a younger household head would now prefer to rent. Although the subgroup of respondents with a household head under 25 was relatively small (58 in 1986, 41 in 1989), the drop in the proportion preferring to rent was dramatic enough to appear significant. It would seem that purchasing their home had become more attractive to this youngest age group over the intervening three years.

56. Those who expected that in five years' time they would be better off than in 1989 were far more likely to prefer to own their own home (89%), than those who expected to be worse off or about the same (62%). Knowing other homeowners was also associated with a preference to own. Of those who said that about half or more of their family and friends owned their home, 80% said they would prefer to own their home, compared to only 55% of those who said that a few, one, or none of their family and friends owned their home. Similarly, of those respondents who knew at least three people who had bought their council home, 80% said they would themselves prefer to own, compared to 68% of those who knew one or two council home buyers, and 52% of those who knew none at all.

Table 13: **Percentage who, if they lived in their ideal home, would prefer to rent rather than own**

By household type	1 adult 16-59	1 adult 60+	2 adults no children	3+ adults no children	1 adult 1 child	2+ adults 1+ child
	36	51	31	18	10	13

By gross weekly household income (£)	up to 58	59-96	97-135	136-230	231+
	45	38	23	17	6

By age of head of household	16-24	25-44	45-64	65-74	75+
	5	11	29	39	54

By length of tenancy (years)	under 5	5-9	10-19	20-29	30+
	15	26	26	28	43

By how many friends and family own home	All or most	About half	A few	One or none
	18	22	37	50

Reasons for Not Purchasing

57. All tenants who were not currently in the process of trying to buy their home (including those who had tried in the past but not gone through with the purchase) were shown a list of 25 potential reasons for deciding not to buy and asked to say which applied to them. The most common reasons mentioned were being worried about affording the repayments (39% of tenants cited this reason), being too old to buy (35%), and being unable to get a loan (32%). However, a sizeable minority (21%) said that they had simply never considered the possibility of buying. The proportion of tenants who perceived themselves to be too old to buy in 1986 was 40%, so it would appear that the perception of being too old had become slightly less common by 1989. This is supported by the observation in paragraph 23 that there had been an increase in purchases by pensioners over this period. The proportions mentioning the other reasons were very similar to those observed in 1986.

Figure 2 **Main reasons for not buying present home**

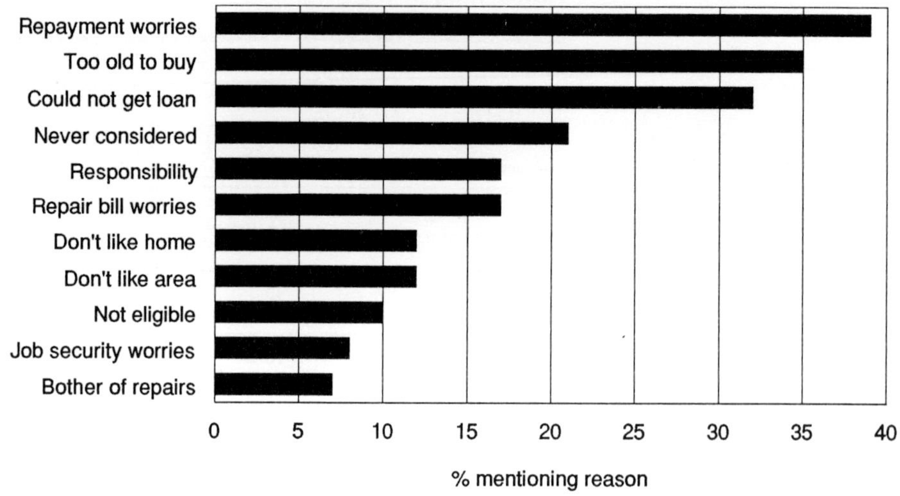

Base: all tenants not currently in process of trying to buy (n=772)

58. When asked to single out the *one* main reason from all the reasons presented, 1 in 5 respondents (21%) said that being 'too old to buy' was the main reason, and nearly as many (19%) picked 'worries about affording the repayments'. 13% chose 'could not get a loan' as the main reason why they were not buying their home. These figures are not significantly different from those found by the 1986 survey: in 1986 the proportion of tenants giving these as their main reasons for not buying were: too old to buy, 22%; worries about repayments, 15%; could not get a loan, 11%.

59. There was a slight difference between tenants of flats and tenants of houses in the main reason they gave for not buying their home. Tenants of flats were more likely to say that they had never considered the possibility of buying (11%) than were tenants of houses (4%), or that they did not like their home (7%, compared to 1% of tenants of houses), and were slightly less likely to give worries about repayments as being their main reason (16% compared to 20% of tenants of houses) or the fact that they could not get a loan (10% compared to 16% of tenants of houses).

Tenants' Expectations of the Future

60. Of all the tenants, only around 1 in 10 (11%) thought that they would ever buy their *current* home. However, 1 in 5 (21%) thought it either 'very likely' or 'fairly likely' that they would *ever* become a homeowner, although over half of those people thought it was either 'very likely' or 'fairly likely' to happen within the next five years.

61. Tenants of houses were twice as likely as tenants of flats to think that they would buy their current home at some stage in the future, but they were no more likely than tenants of flats to think that they would ever become a home owner; 19% of tenants of houses thought that that was either 'very likely' or 'fairly likely', compared to 22% of tenants of flats. Despite the fact that tenants of flats were less likely to expect to buy their current home, but no less likely to expect to ever become homeowners, they were also no less likely to expect to become owners within the next five years.

Table 14. **Percentage thinking it either very or fairly likely that they will . . .**

	All	Tenants Houses	Flats
	%	%	%
Ever buy their current home	11	14	6
Ever become a homeowner	21	19	22
Become a homeowner in the next 5 years	13	12	14
Base	676	422	254

62. Of those who thought it either 'very likely' or 'fairly likely' that they would one day become a homeowner, over 9 out of 10 tenants of houses said that they would not seriously consider buying a flat, as did 6 out of 10 tenants of flats[4]. Only 3% of tenants who thought it either 'very likely' or 'fairly likely' that they would one day become homeowners said that they would not seriously consider buying a house—these were all currently tenants of flats. Of those who would consider a house there was little discrimination between the type of house that they would consider. Semi-detached houses were the most popular—81% said they would consider buying a semi—but other types were not far behind; 64% said they would consider an end-of-terrace house, 62% a detached house, 64% a bungalow and 50% a mid-terrace house.

63. Two thirds (67%) of those who thought it likely that they would become homeowners said that they would seriously consider buying another council home (if they got a transfer). This figure was higher for tenants of flats (82%) than for tenants of houses (57%), a finding which tallies with the observation that more tenants of flats expected to become homeowners although fewer expected to buy their current home.

64. Of all tenants who were either currently in the process of trying to buy their home, or expected to buy it in the future, 20% of tenants of houses and 35% of tenants of flats said that they also seriously considered moving from their current address. An even higher number, 22% of tenants of houses and 50% of tenants of flats, said that if they had a choice they would like to move from the address, but very few (6% overall) said they were on the council's transfer or exchange lists—only half the national average (Department of the Environment, 1988, table 7.22).

65. The same subgroup of respondents were then asked how likely they thought it was that they would one day buy a home other than their current one. Of the 47 respondents who thought it either 'very likely' or 'fairly likely', 1 would only consider buying a flat, 4 would consider buying a flat or a house, 40 would consider only a house, and 2 did not answer. The most popular type of house was semi-detached—36 of the 44 would consider buying one, but there was little difference in popularity between other types; 28 respondents said they would consider a detached house, 26 a bungalow, 22 an end-of-terrace house, and 22 a mid-terrace house.

66. Of the 47 respondents who thought it either 'very likely' or 'fairly likely' that they would one day buy a home other than their current one, 25 said that if they got a transfer they would seriously consider buying another council home,

[4] There were only 22 respondents who said that they *would* seriously consider buying a flat: 18 would consider a purpose-built flat, 9 a flat in a converted house, 3 a flat in a tower block, 19 a flat with a garden, 12 a flat without a garden, and 16 a ground floor flat.

whereas 18 said that they definitely would not. This was a similar pattern to that observed in 1986.

New Buyers' Expectations of the Future

67. Nearly half of the new buyers (41%) said that if they had the choice they would like to move from their current address. The figure was higher among households which contained at least one wage earner (48%) than others (24%), and was lower amongst those who found it easy (or very easy) to afford the total payments for housing (26%) than others (52%).

68. The proportion who would like to move corresponded with the proportion who thought it either very likely or fairly likely that they would one day move from their current address (41%). This figure was itself similar to that found on the 1986 survey (Kerr, 1988, para. 191). The proportion thinking it very or fairly likely that they would one day move was 62% among those who would like to move, and 24% among those who would not like to move. 50% of households containing at least one wage earner thought it either very or fairly likely that they would move, compared to just 15% of those with no wage earners in the household.

69. Of the 33 new buyers who thought it either very or fairly likely that they would move, 9 thought that it would happen within the next two years, 8 thought it might take 3 or 4 years, and 12 thought that it would take at least five years (4 did not know). 31 of the 33 said that if they did move they would *buy* another property, while the other 2 were not sure. However, only one respondent said that they would seriously consider buying a flat, and only 11 said that they would consider buying another council home.

70. 12% of the new buyers (10 respondents) said that if they had the opportunity they would like to become a council tenant again. 9 of these 10 would still consider becoming a tenant even if it meant moving to another home. This would appear to show a major change since 1986, when only 3% of buyers said that they would like to go back to renting, but the finding should be treated as suggestive rather than conclusive, due to the small numbers involved.

71. Only 2 out of 82 new buyers had ever *tried* to sell their current home. (Of these, one had since withdrawn their property from the market, and the other, while still on the market, had not yet been successful.)

72. Nearly three-quarters of the new buyers (72%) thought that it would be either very or fairly easy to sell their home. The figure had been very similar in 1986.

Reasons for Purchasing

73. All tenants who were currently in the process of trying to buy their own home, plus those who expected to buy their current home in the future, and all new buyers, were presented with a set of 17 small cards, each giving a possible reason for buying one's home. They were asked to sort the cards into 3 piles: reasons that were very important, quite important, or not very important to them when deciding whether or not to buy their home. They were then asked to identify the single *most* important reason. The financial advantages of owning and the sense of security that ownership is perceived to give emerged as the major positive considerations.

Figure 3 **Most important reason for buying council home**

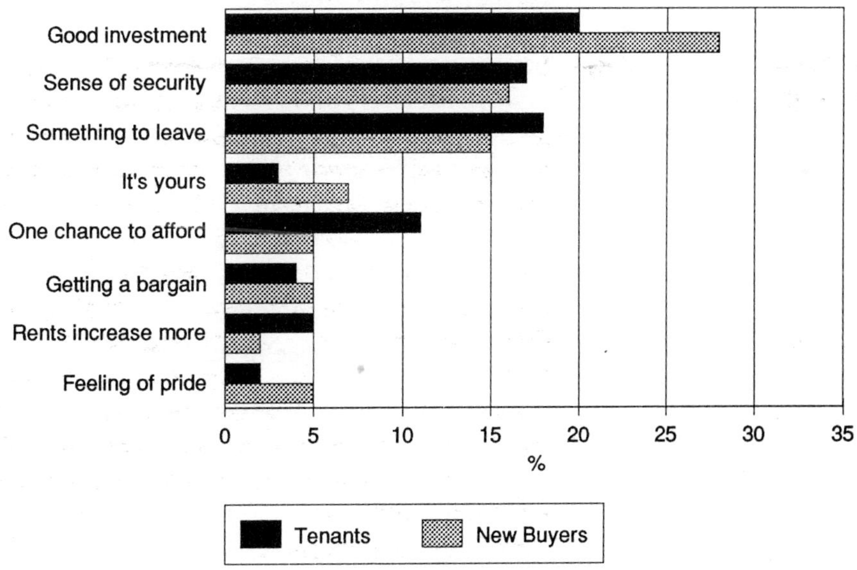

74. Of the reasons presented, the one that was most important to respondents was simply that buying their own home was a good financial investment: three-quarters (76%) said that was 'very important' to them (74% of tenants trying to buy, or who expected to buy, their home, and 79% of new buyers), and 23% said that this was the single most important reason of those offered. The importance of financial considerations was further emphasised by the fact that over half (53%) said that a very important reason in deciding whether to buy was that it was likely to be their only chance to afford to own a home, and even more (58%) thought the fact that they were getting a bargain was very important. (This proportion was 71% among new buyers, and 50% among tenants. The difference may partly be due to people who had actually completed the purchase being more aware of the value-for-money of their purchase and hence overstating its importance to them at the stage of deciding whether to buy.) In 1986, 65% of buyers said the fact that they were getting a bargain was very important, a figure not significantly different from that for the new buyers. 6 out of 10 (63%) said that the purchase of their home giving a sense of security was very important to them, and nearly as many (59%) thought the fact that it was something that was *theirs* was very important. 56% saw the fact that it gave them something to leave to their family as being very important; indeed, 17% said that this was the single most important reason.

75. The freedom obtained, both in terms of being able to do what they like to the property and in terms of being more able to move home afterwards, was seen as a very important factor by around a third of people.

76. Apart from 'getting a bargain' the proportion thinking each reason very important did not vary significantly between the new buyers and the tenants. The exceptions were the 'freedom' issues, which appeared slightly more important to the new buyers: 51% of the new buyers thought that the ability to do what they liked to the property was a very important reason, compared to 42% of tenants. Similarly 52% of the new buyers thought that the ability to do repairs when they liked was an important consideration, compared to 38% of tenants. However, these differences are not statistically significant due to the small bases involved.

77. These same questions were asked in 1986 both of those respondents currently in the process of trying to buy their home, and of those who had already bought. However, it is impossible to compare the current findings with the replies of those who were in the process of buying in 1986, as there were only 18 such respondents at that time. The current findings can, however, be compared with the replies of those who had already bought in 1986, and they turn out to be very similar. There were no real differences between buyers in 1986 and new buyers in 1989 in the proportions thinking each reason very important.

Table 15: **Importance to tenants of reasons in deciding whether or not to buy**

Reasons for deciding to buy council home		Most important reason	Importance of each: Very important	Quite important	Not very important	Mean[5]
Good financial investment	%	20	74	18	8	2.7
Gives sense of security	%	17	62	31	8	2.5
It's something that's yours	%	3	62	29	9	2.5
Likely to be only chance to afford own home	%	11	55	35	9	2.5
Gives you something to leave your family	%	18	53	28	18	2.3
You're getting a bargain	%	4	50	32	18	2.3
Rents increase more than mortgages over the years	%	5	46	35	18	2.3
Gives feeling of pride to own your home	%	2	43	36	20	2.2
Little difference between mortgage and rent	%	2	44	33	23	2.2
Can do what you like to property	%	2	42	40	19	2.2
Can carry out repairs when and how you like	%	1	38	41	22	2.2
Going to live there all life so might as well own it	%	5	42	22	36	2.1
Can use as stepping stone to better home	%	5	37	40	23	2.1
Gives freedom to move	%	5	37	29	40	1.9
Have already done a lot to property	%	1	31	24	46	1.9
Having spare money to invest	%	0	23	31	46	1.8
Council not maintaining property properly	%	0	14	23	63	1.5

Table 16: **Importance to new buyers of reasons in deciding whether or not to buy**

Reasons for deciding to buy council home		Most important reason	Importance of each: Very important	Quite important	Not very important	Mean[5]
Good financial investment	%	28	79	12	5	2.7
Gives sense of security	%	16	66	30	4	2.6
It's something that's yours	%	7	54	40	6	2.5
Likely to be only chance to afford own home	%	5	50	35	15	2.4
Gives you something to leave your family	%	15	62	23	15	2.5
You're getting a bargain	%	5	71	23	6	2.6
Rents increase more than mortgages over the years	%	2	45	29	26	2.2
Gives feeling of pride to own your home	%	5	51	35	13	2.4
Little difference between mortgage and rent	%	1	32	32	37	2.0
Can do what you like to property	%	1	51	34	15	2.4
Can carry out repairs when and how you like	%	0	52	33	15	2.4
Going to live there all life so might as well own it	%	2	43	28	29	2.1
Can use as stepping stone to better home	%	4	38	22	40	2.0
Gives freedom to move	%	5	34	30	35	2.0
Have already done a lot to property	%	0	29	29	43	1.9
Having spare money to invest	%	0	17	27	56	1.6
Council not maintaining property properly	%	1	18	23	59	1.6

[5] Mean calculated by assigning a score of 3 to 'very important', 2 to 'quite important' and 1 to 'not very important'.

Changes which might increase the Likelihood of Purchase

78. All the tenants not currently in the process of buying their home were asked whether each of seven possible changes might increase the likelihood of them buying their home in the future. (Respondents who had said that they did not expect to ever buy their current home were asked whether the change would make them likely to consider buying, whereas those who *did* expect to buy their current home were asked whether the change would influence them to start the buying process.) This was a new question, not asked in the 1986 survey. The changes were hypothetical and replies cannot be used to make predictions of possible levels of take-up if the changes really did happen. The replies should be interpreted as indicating the relative interest generated by the different ideas.

79. For each of the seven possible changes the differences between subgroups showed a similar *pattern,* although there were significant differences in the overall *level* of interest generated by each change. This suggests that to a large extent the differences observed between subgroups are independent of the particular change being considered: certain subgroups are perhaps more likely than others to consider buying their home under *any* circumstances. The findings described throughout this section suggest that these sub-groups are households with children, households with a young head-of-household, households with higher incomes and, to a lesser extent, households headed by a male. Many of these factors are of course correlated with one another, e.g. the existence of children in the household and the age of the head of household, so a multivariate analysis was carried out to examine the *relative* effects of each of these variables. This analysis concluded that most of the observed differences can be explained by differences in the age of the head-of-household, the household composition, and the type of property (those in houses were more likely than those in flats or maisonettes to think that changes might make them consider buying their home). After allowing for these variables, household income, and sex of head-of-household provided no further discrimination. (Appendix C contains a technical summary of this multivariate analysis.)

80. The findings reported in this section also suggest that there exist other subgroups of tenants who are largely resolved and/or resigned to renting, and who would thus be fairly impervious to attempts to persuade them to buy. These subgroups appear to include people living alone, households with an older head of household, and households on a low income (variables which are correlated with one another).

Improvement in Financial Position

81. The first change suggested was an improvement in the respondent's financial situation. Half the tenants of houses (51%) thought that such an improvement might make them likely to consider buying their home, but less than a quarter (22%) of tenants of flats thought that.

82. The proportion thinking that an improvement in their financial situation might make them likely to consider buying their home was higher amongst households containing children (54%) than amongst those without children (35%). Furthermore, amongst households containing children it was higher if there were at least two adults in the household (60%) than if there was a single parent (38%), and amongst those without children it was higher the more adults there were: 28% of single people, 38% of 2-adult households, and 53% of households containing 3 or more adults. Tenants in households headed by a male (46%) were slightly more likely than those in households headed by a female (34%) to think that an improvement in their financial situation might make them likely to consider buying.

83. The proportion was also larger the greater the household's gross weekly income—29% of those with a weekly income of £96 or less, 53% of those with incomes between £97 and £154, and 66% of those with greater incomes. This finding suggests that respondents were thinking realistically in terms of the sorts of improvements that would be likely to happen, in so far as a relatively small improvement in finances is more likely to enable the household to buy their property the better their finances are in the first place. It also suggests that lack of finances are a major obstacle to purchase, as even amongst the top income bracket two-thirds thought that an improvement in finances might make them more likely to purchase. This correlates with the findings reported in paragraphs 57 to 59 that some of the most common reasons for not purchasing were those associated with finance.

84. Multivariate analysis showed that households with a head aged between 25 and 44, those consisting of two adults with no children, and those living in a house (rather than a flat or maisonette) were more likely than others to consider buying if their financial situation improved. After allowing for the effect of these variables, no significant differences remained between households of different compositions, those in different types of house, or between households with different levels of income, or with heads of different sex. However, this multivariate analysis was confined to those who did not expect to buy their current home (for reasons explained in Appendix C), relatively few of whom were households with children. Those who did not expect to buy their home, but had children, were *less* likely than others to think that an improvement in their financial position might make them consider buying. Overall, however, households with children were *more* likely to already think that they would one day buy their current home.

Change in Family Situation

85. Only 12% of tenants thought that a change in their family situation (e.g. more or fewer people living with them) might increase the likelihood of them buying their home. The figure was higher for tenants of houses (15%) than tenants of flats (7%).

86. It was higher for households containing children (16%) than for those without (11%). Among single-person households it was higher the younger the respondent: 21% of those aged 16-59, 10% of those aged 60-69, and just 3% of those age 70 or over thought that such a change might make a difference.

87. The figure did not vary between households headed by males and those headed by females, but it did seem to be related to the age of the head of the household: it was 14% amongst households with a head aged under 35, 29% amongst those with a head aged between 35 and 44, 14% amongst those with a head aged between 45 and 64, and just 4% amongst those with a head of household aged 65 or over.

88. Multivariate analysis suggested that, amongst those who did not expect to one day buy their current home, living in a house (rather than a flat), and having a household head aged between 25 and 44, increased the respondent's propensity to say that a change in their family situation might make them consider buying, whereas household composition, and level of income, did not significantly affect the propensity.

Improvements or Repairs to the Home

89. Respondents did not generally think that they would be influenced to buy if the council carried out improvements or repairs to their home. Only 23% of tenants in houses and 13% of tenants in flats thought that this might increase their propensity to buy their home.

90. Again there were differences between sub-groups, however. The proportion thinking that the council carrying out improvements or repairs to the home might make them likely to purchase was 34% among households with children, 16% among households consisting of two or more adults but with no children and just 8% among single-person households; it was 32% among households where the head of household was aged under 55, and 8% among those with an older head of household; it was 37% among households with a gross weekly income greater than £192, 26% among those with an income between £97 and £192, and 13% among those with a lower income. Again, multivariate analysis suggested that the effect of household income was not significant after allowing for property type and age of head-of-household.

Improvements in the Area

91. An even less enthusiastic response was given to the idea that improvements in the area around the home might increase the likelihood to buy: only 16% of tenants of houses and 10% of tenants of flats agreed, although again there were differences between subgroups, similar to those observed in paragraph 90. The proportion thinking that improvements in the area might make them likely to purchase was 23% among households with children, 14% among households consisting of two or more adults (no children), and just 6% among single-person households; it was 24% among households where the head of household was aged under 55, and 6% among those with an older head of household; it was 30% among households with a gross weekly income greater than £192, 20% among those with an income between £97 and £192, and 8% among those with a lower income. Again, multivariate analysis suggested that the most important discriminators were age of head-of-household, and property type.

Continuing Rent Rises

92. Interestingly, a quarter (25%) of the tenants of houses thought that they might be likely to consider buying their home if the rent continued to rise at about the same rate as in 1989, although only 11% of tenants of flats thought this. It is difficult to know how best to interpret this. The average local authority rent rise in England between April 1988 and April 1989 was estimated to be 9.6% (Chartered Institute of Public Finance and Accountancy, 1989). This was only slightly above the increase in the Retail Price Index over the same period (8.0%[6], HMSO, 1989, table 18.1), and the estimated increase in average earnings (9.1%, HMSO, 1989, table 18.10). Furthermore the increase in average mortgage interest repayments over this period was much higher, at 54.2%[7], suggesting that the level of rent rises would not be expected to act as an incentive to purchase ones home. Consequently the finding that a substantial proportion of tenants thought that they might be likely to consider buying their home if the rent continued to rise at about the same rate as in 1989 seemed somewhat illogical. However, it may well be that respondents felt their pockets were hard hit by the rent increases in recent years (the increases in the years to April 1988 and April 1989 were certainly much higher than in the previous two years) without having considered or indeed being aware that mortgage payments had been increasing at a much greater rate. A check was

[6]But caution must be expressed when comparing LA rent rises to the R.P.I. as housing costs overall (including mortgage repayments, rates, private rents, etc) themselves have a strong influence on the R.P.I. The increase in the R.P.I. *excluding housing* in the year to April 1989 was only 5.3%.

[7]This figure was obtained by taking the ratio of the R.P.I. for mortgage interest payments in April 1989 (HMSO, 1989, table 18.2) with that for April 1988 (e.g. HMSO, 1988, table 18.2).

made to see whether the survey respondents had experienced higher-than-average rent increases, but this seemed not to be the case: the Spring 1989 Survey of Rent and Housing Benefits (CIPFA, 1989) shows that 27 of the 366 LAs in England (7.4%) reported average rent increases of £3-50 or more. Only 2 of these 27 are among the 40 LAs covered by the survey, accounting for 7.4% of the issued addresses.

93. The proportion thinking they might consider buying their home if the rent continued to rise at about the same rate as in 1989 was greater among households containing children, households with a young head of household, those with a male head of household, and those with higher incomes. It was 35% among households containing children, 16% among households consisting of two or more adults (no children), and 8% among single-person households; it was 34% among households headed by someone aged under 55, and 8% among those with an older head of household; it was 24% among households with a male head, and 14% among those with a female head; it was 46% among households with a gross-weekly income greater than £192, 27% among those with an income between £97 and £192, and 11% among those with a lower income. Multivariate analysis showed the effects of property type, household composition, and age of head-of-household, to be significant, but not sex of head-of-household, or household income.

Transferral to a New Landlord

94. The prospect of transferring the home to a new landlord, rather than the council, was not seen a being likely to make the respondent consider buying their home; only 17% of tenants of houses and 10% of tenants of flats thought that it might. Again this proportion was higher among households containing children, households with a young head, households headed by a male, and those with higher incomes, although multivariate analysis suggested that the latter two factors were not, in fact, significant.

Purchase at same Cost as Rent

95. The importance of financial considerations was again evident as half of the tenants of houses (49%) said that they would be likely to consider buying their house if they could buy it without paying out more than they were presently paying in rent. A quarter (24%) of the tenants of flats also thought that under these circumstances they would be likely to consider purchasing, so, of the seven possible changes, this was the one scenario most likely to increase the number of tenants of flats wanting to buy their home. Among certain subgroups the proportion likely to consider purchasing their home if they could buy it without paying out more than they currently paid in rent reached a sizeable majority, viz 61% of households containing children (compared to 35% of households consisting of two or more adults with no children, and 25% of single-person households), 59% of households headed by someone aged under 55 (and 71% of households headed by someone aged between 35 and 44), and 69% of households with a gross weeekly income of £155 or more.

96. Multivariate analysis of those who did not expect to buy their home suggested that the significant factors in discriminating between those who did, and those who did not, think that they would consider buying if they could buy without paying out more than they were presently paying in rent, were property type (living in a house, rather than a flat or maisonette, increased the propensity to consider buying), age of head of household (those aged 25 to 44 had a higher propensity), and household composition (households consisting of two adults and no children had a greater propensity).

4. Income and Housing Costs

97. This chapter examines the relationship between the income received by households and the amount they had to pay for their housing.

Tenants' Housing Costs

98. The mean weekly amount paid out for rent and rates by tenant households in the sample, *after* any housing benefit received, was £19.41. The mean was £20.83 for tenants of houses and £16.74 for tenants of flats. This compares with a national average of £20.62 *prior* to any housing benefit, as at the end of April 1989 (CIPFA, 1989).

Table 17: **Weekly rent and rates, after any housing benefit**

	Tenants		
	All	Houses	Flats
	%	%	%
0	2	1	3
£1-£4	22	21	26
£5-£9	13	12	16
£10-£19	13	12	14
£20-£29	15	14	17
£30-£39	29	33	21
£40+	5	7	4
Mean	£19.41	£20.83	£16.74
Base	775	505	270

99. The amount paid out weekly in rent and rates was, not surprisingly, higher for larger households than for smaller ones. Households with two or more adults and at least one child paid twice as much (£26.03 on average) as single person households (£12.67). Households with 3 or more adults but no children paid even more (£28.65).

100. The amount paid in rent and rates was higher when the head of household was middle-aged and lowest when they were over 75. Households headed by a male paid an average of £23.19, and those headed by a female an average of £13.58.

101. The average weekly amount paid out was £17.71 in the north and £21.39 in the south of the country[8].

Table 18: **Average weekly rent and rates after any housing benefit**

By household type	1 Adult 16–59	1 Adult 60+	2 Adults No children	3+ Adults No children	1 Adult 1+ child	2+ Adults 1+ child
	£16.59	£11.07	£22.10	£28.65	£8.56	£26.03
By age of head of household	16–34	35–54	55–64	65–74	75+	
	£19.75	£24.25	£18.86	£17.66	£13.14	

[8] The south is defined as the following four standards regions: Greater London, South East, South West, and East Anglia.

102. These differences observed for subgroups are partly explained by differences in property type (eg. larger households occupy larger homes, which command higher rents) and partly explained by differences in the level of housing benefit received (eg. single parents tend to receive more housing benefit than couples, and hence pay out less in rent).

New Buyers' Housing Costs

103. Whereas for tenants the cost of housing was simply rent and rates, for buyers the situation was more complicated. Their regular payments were likely to include any or all of the following: repayments of mortgage or loan; premiums on an endowment policy linked to a mortgage; rent to the council on a percentage of the property; rates (including water rates); buildings insurance; premiums on a mortgage protection policy; service charges. The sum of all these payments can be considered the 'total housing costs'. Figure 4 shows the proportion of new buyers having to make each of those types of payment.

Figure 4 **Payments made by new buyers**

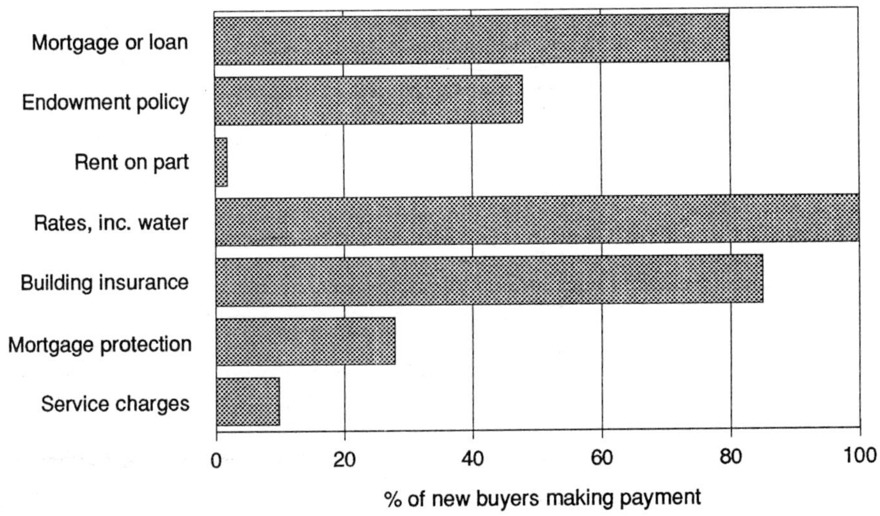

104. The mean weekly total housing cost among new buyers, after any housing benefit, was £48.33. This figure was nearly 2.5 times the mean rent and rates paid by tenants. However, it has already been seen that new buying households had, on average, more adults, more wage-earners, and larger properties than tenants, all characteristics that, even among tenants, correlate with higher housing costs. It is likely that these characteristics were also correlated with housing costs among new buyers.[9]

105. At the aggregate level nearly two-thirds (63%) of the new buyers' total housing costs were accounted for by repayments on mortgages or loans, and a further 12% by the premiums on endowment policies linked to mortgages. However, the rates (including water rates) still accounted for a substantial one-fifth (20%) of total housing costs. The remainder of the costs were buildings insurance (3%), premiums on mortgage protection policies (1%), service charges (1%), and rent on a percentage of the property (−).

Housing Benefit—Tenants

106. Over half of the tenant households (56%) received some housing benefit, a figure which is very similar to the 1988 national average of 59% reported by CIPFA, 1989. The proportion was slightly higher for tenants of flats (61%) than for tenants of houses (53%). A slightly higher proportion of the sample

[9] But no analysis of housing costs by subgroups of new buyers is possible due to the small numbers involved.

had been receiving housing benefit or rent rebate at the time of the 1986 survey—65% of tenants of flats, and 57% of tenants of houses (58% overall).

107. Those who did receive some housing benefit subsequently paid out an average of £9.66 a week for rent and rates, whereas those who received nothing paid an average of £31.88.

108. Very high proportions of single-parent households (91%) and of people over 60 living alone (84%) received housing benefit. Just over half (55%) the people aged 16—59 living alone received it, as did half (50%) of households consisting of two adults (no children). Even amongst households containing 3 or more adults but no children nearly 1 in 3 (29%) were in receipt of housing benefit.

109. The relationship between the receipt of housing benefit and the age of the head of household was almost identical to that of the amount of rent and rates paid out; those who paid out the most, households with heads aged between 35 and 54, received the lowest level of housing benefit, only 41% getting any at all, whereas 77% of households with heads aged 75 or more (those who paid out the least in rent and rates) received some housing benefit. Similarly, three-quarters (76%) of households headed by a female received housing benefit, compared to less than half (44%) of households headed by a male.

110. Slightly more households in the north (59%) than in the south (54%) received housing benefit[10].

Table 19: **Percentage of Tenant Households Receiving Housing Benefit**

By household type	1 adult 16-59	1 adult 60+	2 adults No children	3+ adults No children	1 adult 1+ child	2+ adults 1+ child
	55	84	50	29	91	35
By age of head of household	**16-34**	**35-54**	**55-64**	**65-74**	**75+**	
	51	41	59	67	77	

Housing Benefit—New Buyers

111. Less than 1 in 7 (13%) of the new buyers received some housing benefit (compared to four times that proportion of tenants—see para. 106). Amongst those who did receive it, the average amount received was just £3.64 per week. Consequently this low level of housing benefit receipt would seem to be another contributory factor to the difference in housing costs for tenants and new buyers reported in para. 104.

112. The proportion of new buyers receiving housing benefit is similar to the proportion of buyers receiving housing benefit in 1986, when the figure was 10%.

Levels of Income

113. The questionnaire did not attempt to make a precise estimate of each household's income. Instead it asked the respondent to choose the income range which corresponded to the household's total weekly income from all sources, before tax and other deductions, from those listed on a show card.

[10]The south is defined as the following four standard regions: Greater London, South East, South West, and East Anglia.

114. Not surprisingly new buying households tended to have higher incomes than tenant households. Gross weekly household income from all sources amounted to no more than £115 for 63% of the tenant households, but only 27% of the new buying households had such a low income[11] . 52% of new buying households had a gross weekly household income of over £230, compared with only 11% of tenant households. It is not possible to compare household income with 1986 figures because of the different method of obtaining the data, and because of the effects of inflation.

115. Because of the banded nature of the income data it is not possible to estimate *mean* gross weekly household income, but the *median* weekly income was found to be just under £100. Median income was much lower for tenants of flats (about £75) than for tenants of houses (about £105). Indeed, only 25% of tenants of flats estimated their gross weekly household income to be over £115, whereas 42% of tenants of houses exceeded this figure.

Table 20: **Gross Weekly Household Income from all Sources**

	TENANTS			
	All	Houses	Flats	New Buyers
	%	%	%	%
Less than £39	4	1	8	1
£39-£58	18	13	27	7
£59-£77	15	15	16	4
£78-£96	15	16	14	4
£97-£115	11	11	9	11
£116-£154	13	15	9	9
£155-£230	13	16	7	12
£231 +	11	11	9	52
Base	735	480	255	81

Earners in the household

116. The low levels of income observed are undoubtedly due to a large proportion of households having to rely upon benefits and allowances of various sorts. Well over half the tenant households (58%) contained no wage earners at all; the proportion was higher for tenants of flats (68%) than for tenants of houses (53%). Only 22% of tenant households in houses contained two or more wage earners, as did only 9% of tenant households in flats.

117. New buying households, being larger and less likely to contain pensioners, had more wage earners than tenant households, but fewer than pre-1986 buying households. Only 13% of pre-1986 buying households contained no wage-earners, whereas the figure was 22% amongst the new buyers. Nevertheless this is well below the 58% of tenant households that contained no wage earners. Conversely over half of new-buying households contained at least two wage earners, compared with only 17% of tenant households.

Savings

118. Less than half of the tenant respondents had any savings of any kind. The proportion was little different for tenants of houses (43%) and tenants of flats (40%). Of those who did have savings, 57% of tenants of houses and 45% of

[11]Figures from the 1988 FES showed a similar pattern, though they are not strictly comparable due to the difference in time, the different income bands used, and the fact that they do not separate out RTB purchasers from other owner-occupiers. Nevertheless, they showed that 80% of council tenant households had a gross weekly income under £100, compared to 34% of owner-occupiers in the process of purchasing (Central Statistical Office, 1990, table 26).

tenants of flats said that they amounted to over £1000, and 6 out of 10 (62% of tenants of houses and 59% of tenants of flats) had at least some of their savings in a building society account.

119. The overall proportion with savings in 1989 was slightly lower than that found in 1986. At that time 45% of tenants of houses and 44% of tenants of flats reported having savings. Of those who had savings, the proportion who had at least some of them in a building society account had risen from 50% to 61% between 1986 and 1989.

Security of Income

120. Two-thirds of tenants in households that had at least one person in paid work thought that their household's income was either very secure or fairly secure. A quarter thought that it was either not very secure or not at all secure, and the rest were not sure. The proportion thinking that the household's income was either very or fairly secure was 71% in the south and 67% in the north, and was slightly higher in households with two or more wage earners (75%) than those with only one (65%).

121. New buyers were much more confident about the security of their income. Amongst new buying households with at least one person in paid work, more than 9 out of 10 thought their income was either very or fairly secure.

Expectations of future Income

122. Among tenants there was not a great deal of optimism about future improvements in income. Less than a third (30%) expected to be better off in five years' time, a third (34%) expected little change, and nearly a quarter (22%) expected to be worse off. Optimism was higher among new buyers: nearly half (44%) expected to be better off, and over a quarter (29%) expected little change, although 1 in 5 (20%) expected to be worse off. These results were broadly similar to the 1986 findings, when buyers were again more optimistic than tenants.

Difficulties in paying for housing

123. Respondents were asked how easy or difficult they found it to make the total payments for housing. Tenants split approximately equally between those who found it easy to afford (33%), those who found it neither easy nor difficult (36%), and those who found it difficult (30%). The proportion who reported difficulties was slightly greater than the proportion of tenants who had reported having difficulties in 1986 (25%), but the proportion finding it easy to afford payments for housing had altered little, having been 34% in 1986.

124. Fewer new buyers than tenants reported difficulties in making the payments for housing (6%), but no more found it easy (38%). The proportion of tenants reporting difficulties in making the payments for housing was 48% among those who felt that their household's income was either not very or not at all secure, 23% of those who felt it was fairly secure, and 18% of those who thought it very secure.

125. The proportion who reported having difficulties making the payments for housing varied little by household type. This suggests that the system of paying housing benefit was to some extent successful in 'softening the blow' for those with particular hardships. It is certainly true that many people who received housing benefit did not perceive the payments for housing as being difficult to afford. For example, among single parent tenant households, over 90% of whom received housing benefit, only 30% said that they had difficulties in paying for their housing. Similarly, despite the differences observed in rent levels and receipt of housing benefit, the age of the head of household had little effect on the proportion finding it difficult to pay for their housing. Also,

similar proportions of households headed by males (30%) and those headed by females (31%) found payments difficult. Revealingly, the proportion finding payments difficult was the same for those who did receive housing benefit as for those who did not.

Table 21: **Percentage of Tenants finding it Difficult to Afford the Payments for Housing**

By Household Type	1 Adult 16-59	1 Adult 60+	2 Adults No children	3+ Adults No children	1 Adult 1+ child	2+ Adults 1+ child
	38	29	34	26	30	27
By Age of Head of Household	**16-34**	**35-54**	**55-64**	**65-74**	**75+**	
	29	34	25	34	30	

The Relationship between Income and Rent

126. There was a very clear relationship between gross weekly household income and the amount that tenant households pay out in rent and rates; the greater the income, the larger the amount of rent and rates. Indeed the data suggested that the *proportion* of income that was spent on rent and rates could be fairly constant across income bands. For example, the average amount paid out in rent and rates by households with a gross income of £116-£154 per week was nearly twice that for households with incomes of £59-£77. The average amount paid by households with an income of over £230 was over four times that for households with an income of £58 or less.

127. Conversely, as one would expect, the proportion of households receiving housing benefit dropped dramatically as gross weekly household income increased. Within each income band the proportion of households receiving housing benefit was very similar to the proportion actually paying out less than £20 per week on rent and rates. Indeed, 96% of tenant households paying out less than £20 per week for rent and rates were in receipt of housing benefit, compared to just 16% of those paying out more.

Table 22: **The Relationship between Rent and Income**

	Gross weekly household income (£)						
Weekly rent & rates paid (after housing benefit)	<58	59-77	78-96	97-115	116-154	155-230	231+
	%	%	%	%	%	%	%
Up to £4	53	32	30	17	16	3	1
£5 - £9	21	21	17	13	8	1	3
£10 - £19	17	21	19	13	6	9	1
£20 - £29	3	14	19	30	.13	21	16
£30 - £39	5	8	16	26	49	57	59
£40+	2	3	1	–	6	10	20
Mean (£)	8.18	12.57	14.67	19.75	24.41	30.33	33.00
Percent of households receiving housing benefit	90	84	78	56	37	13	6
Base	160	113	113	78	97	95	79

Table 23: **The Relationship between Rent and receipt of Housing Benefit**

	Weekly rent and rates paid (after housing benefit)					
	Up to £4	*£5 - £9*	*£10 - £19*	*£20 - £29*	*£30 - £39*	*£40+*
Percentage receiving housing benefit	96	99	93	31	8	14
Base	188	101	99	118	223	45

128. Although the gross weekly household income was only obtained in banded form, the actual gross pay of the respondent and/or spouse was also obtained if either or both were in paid employment. This information allows a limited analysis of the relationship between housing costs and pay. It appears from this that, among tenants, those with lower gross weekly household incomes spent a higher proportion of their pay on rent and rates. Overall, for about two-thirds of tenant households with at least one wage-earner their rent and rates amounted to between 10% and 29% of the gross pay. Similar analysis of total housing costs as a proportion of income was not possible for the new buyers due to the small number for whom the relevant information was forthcoming.

Table 24: **Rent and Rates as a proportion of Gross Pay (Respondent and Spouse)**

Rent and rates as a % of gross pay	Total		Gross weekly household income Less than £155	£155+
	%	%	%	%
0	1	2	4	0
1-4	1	2	4	1
5-9	2	7	5	10
10-19	14	41	18	57
20-29	8	25	34	19
30-39	3	9	15	4
40-49	2	6	7	4
50+	3	9	14	5
No pay	66			
Base (all tenants)	727			
Base (all with pay)		244	103	134

5. Maintenance and Repairs

129. The report of the 1986 survey challenged the view that RTB purchasers tend to make improvements to their home that are merely cosmetic and that major maintenance needs might be neglected. The survey found that the majority of buyers were undertaking a significant level of maintenance work. It was also reported that the buyers had done slightly more work *prior* to purchase than had tenants.

130. This chapter compares the levels of maintenance undertaken by new buyers with those of tenants, and with those of pre-1986 buyers. As in the 1986 survey, the level of repairs and improvements that buyers had carried out while still tenants was found to be slightly higher than the level reported by current tenants, but these levels were little different from those found in 1986.

131. A lot of repair and improvement work had been carried out by the new buyers since purchase, and more was planned for the next year or so. However, a substantial minority of new buyers said that there was some repair or improvement work which needed doing to their home but was unlikely to get done in the next year or so. The main reason for this was an inability to afford it.

Satisfaction with the State of Repair of the Home

132. Respondents were asked how satisfied they felt about:

a) the state of repair inside their home;
b) the state of repair of the outside of their house/block;
c) the way the council repairs and maintains their home.

In the case of tenants this satisfaction related to the current time, whereas for buyers it related to the time before they bought.

133. On all three counts large minorities were dissatisfied, but the level of dissatisfaction among tenants with the way the council repaired and maintained the home was slightly lower than that reported by tenants in 1986, and the level of dissatisfaction among new buyers with the council repair and maintenance service prior to purchase was slightly lower than that among buyers in 1986. In both 1986 and 1989 the level of satisfaction on this count was higher among tenants than buyers, but this is partly accounted for by the fact that buyers were referring to a period in the past, and, at least for this sample, satisfaction seems to be increasing over time.

Tenants' Satisfaction

134. Two thirds (66%) of tenants were either satisfied or very satisfied with the state of repair inside their home. A quarter (24%) were either dissatisfied or very dissatisfied. There was no difference between tenants of houses and tenants of flats. In 1986 61% had been either satisfied or very satisfied, and 28% had been either dissatisfied or very dissatisfied.

135. Nearly two-thirds (63%) were either satisfied or very satisfied with the state of repair of the outside of their home, 4% more than in 1986, while nearly

a third (29%) were either dissatisfied or very dissatisfied, just 1% less than in 1986. Again, these proportions were the same for both tenants of houses and tenants of flats.

136. The general level of satisfaction with the way the council repaired and maintained the property was lower than the levels of satisfaction with the state of repair. Only just over half the tenants (54%) were either satisfied or very satisfied, and 1 in 3 (33%) were either dissatisfied or very dissatisfied. Slightly fewer (47%) had been satisfied in 1986, and slightly more (39%) dissatisfied.

Table 25: **Tenants' Satisfaction with the State of Repair and the Council's Repair Service**

	State of repair inside	State of repair outside	Council's repair service
	%	%	%
Very satisfied	20	13	16
Satisfied	46	51	38
Neither satisfied nor dissatisfied	10	8	11
Dissatisfied	17	17	20
Very Dissatisfied	7	12	13
Base	822	822	822

New Buyers' Satisfaction

137. Three quarters (76%) of new buyers recalled being either satisfied or very satisfied with the state of repair inside their home prior to purchase. This was little different to the proportion of buyers who in 1986 recalled satisfaction (72%), but was slightly higher than the proportion of tenants expressing satisfaction in 1989 (66%) and in 1986 (61%).

138. Two thirds (66%) of the new buyers said that they were either satisfied or very satisfied with the state of repair of the outside of their home prior to purchase. This was little different to the proportion of buyers who in 1986 recalled satisfaction prior to purchase (63%), and the proportion of tenants expressing satisfaction in 1989 (63%), but was slightly higher than the proportion of tenants who had been satisfied in 1986 (59%).

139. Less than half (47%) of the new buyers recalled being either satisfied or very satisfied with the way the council repaired and maintained the property prior to purchase, but this was slightly higher than the proportion of buyers who in 1986 recalled satisfaction prior to purchase (38%). These figures were slightly lower than the proportion of tenants who were satisfied (54% in 1989, and 47% in 1986).

Table 26: **New Buyers' Satisfaction with the State of Repair prior to Purchase and the Council's Repair Service**

	State of repair inside	State of repair outside	Council's repair service
	%	%	%
Very satisfied	15	11	7
Satisfied	61	55	40
Neither satisfied nor dissatisfied	11	15	12
Dissatisfied	11	15	27
Very dissatisfied	2	5	14
Base	82	82	81

Repairs and improvements carried out at the tenants' expense

Tenants' Repairs and Improvements

140. Nearly half (45%) of the tenants of houses, but less than a third (29%) of the tenants of flats had carried out any repairs or improvements to their home at their own expense. The figure for the tenants of houses is slightly lower than that reported in the 1986 survey, 54%.

141. Amongst those who had carried out some repairs or improvements the average number of different repairs of improvements undertaken was 2·2 for tenants of houses (compared to 2·4 in 1986) and 1·9 for tenants of flats. The improvement most commonly mentioned was installation of new kitchen units or worktops, nearly 1 in 5 (18%) having done this. Other relatively common improvements were installation of new bathroom units (7%), and installation of central heating (5%). Some tenants had carried out major improvements such as roof or wall insulation (1%), and installation of double-glazing (1%). A number of tenants had also carried out major maintenance work at their own expense, such as replumbing (4%), rewiring (1%), replacement or repair of windows (3%), and replacing the floors or floorboards (3%). 9% had done some replastering.

142. For nearly all of the different types of improvement mentioned, the proportion of tenants of houses reporting having done it was a very slight decrease on the 1986 figure whereas for tenants of flats the proportion had increased slightly. For example, the proportion having installed new kitchen units or worktops had fallen from 25% to 21% of tenants of houses, but risen from 11% to 13% of tenants of flats, and the proportion having replastered at their own expense had dropped from 13% to 11% of tenants of houses, but risen from 4% to 6% of tenants of flats.

New Buyers' Repairs and Improvements prior to purchase

143. Just over half (56%) of the new buyers had carried out some repairs or improvements to their home at their own expense prior to purchasing it, a figure similar to that reported by buyers in 1986 (58%).

144. Amongst those who had carried out some repairs or improvements the average number of different repairs or improvements undertaken was 2·7, no different from that reported by buyers in 1986 (2·6). The most common improvement was, as with tenants, the installation of new kitchen units or worktops (34%), followed by the installation of central heating (11%), installing new bathroom units (10%), and replacing the front door (12%).

Other major improvements included roof or wall insulation (7%), installation of double-glazing (4%), and the building of an extension (7%) or garage (2%). Major maintenance work carried out while still tenants included replumbing (9%), rewiring (4%), replacement or repair of windows (5%), major roof repairs (1%), and repointing (6%). Replastering of walls or ceilings had been carried out by 13%.

145. Virtually all of these proportions are slightly higher than the proportion of tenants reporting having done such work at their own expense (see para. 141), but are very similar to the proportions that buyers in 1986 reported having done while still tenants.

Repairs and improvements carried out since purchase

146. Not only had the new buyers made more repairs and improvements to their home while still tenants than had current tenants, but they had also done significant amounts of work since purchase. More than 9 out of 10 of those who had bought in the period 1985-87, and three-quarters of those who had bought in 1988 or 1989 had carried out some repairs or improvements since purchase, the most common being the installation of new units in the kitchen (35%) or bathroom (20%), replacing the front door (28%), installing central heating (21%), replacing or repairing windows (21%), and installing double-glazing (21%). Other repairs and improvements carried out since purchase included rewiring (9%), replumbing (5%), major roof repairs (2%), roof or wall insulation (5%), building an extension (7%) or garage (1%), repointing (10%), replacing or repairing guttering or drainpipes (10%), and replacing floors or floorboards (2%). One third of new buyers (34%) had redecorated the outside of their home since purchase.

147. Collectively, the level of major repair and maintenance work carried out by the new buyers both before and after purchase would appear to constitute a major effort to maintain a good standard of housing.

148. In addition to the work that the new buyers had already carried out, 62% of them planned to do some in the next year or so. About half planned to install new kitchen units or worktops (51%) or new bathroom units (44%). Fruition of these plans would mean that virtually all new buyers would, at some stage, have installed new kitchen units, and around two-thirds would have installed new bathroom units. Many new buyers also planned to replace the front door (18%), replace or repair windows (13%), replace interior doors (12%), or fit double glazing (9%). Other plans mentioned included repointing (6%), replacing or repairing guttering or drainpipes (6%), installing central heating (5%), building a new porch (10%), garage (7%), or extension (7%), replacing floors or floorboards (4%), replumbing (2%), roof repairs (2%), and roof or wall insulation (2%).

149. However, nearly one third of the new buyers said that there was some repair or improvement work which needed doing to their home but was unlikely to get done in the next year or so. Most of these things were in fact improvements—new bathroom units (7%), new kitchen units (5%), installation of double glazing (4%), installation of central heating (2%), building an extension (4%) or garage (1%)—but there were also some important repairs unlikely to get done—major roof repairs (4%), repointing (5%), replacing or repairing guttering or drainpipes (2%), rewiring (1%), damp-proofing (1%), and external decoration (2%). The most common reason given for these works being unlikely to get done was simply being unable to afford it.

6. New Buyers' Experiences of Purchasing Their Home

150. It seems plausible that the process of buying one's home could seem confusing and complicated to many council tenants, the majority of whom will be first-time buyers. (In the present survey 83% of new buyers said that neither they nor their spouse had ever owned another property they lived in). This did indeed appear to be the case as over a third (35%) of the new buyers said that they had found the buying process 'very difficult', and the majority of the remainder found it 'fairly difficult'. Less than 1 in 7 (14%) found it either very easy or fairly easy.

151. Nevertheless, the difficulties appear to have been worthwhile as the vast majority of new buyers (96%) said that taking everything into account they were pleased that they had bought their council home.

Basis of ownership

152. 90% of the new buyers owned the freehold of their property while 10% owned on a leasehold basis. None said that they purchased through a shared ownership scheme (although 2 out of the 82 new buyers reported paying rent on part of the property, so those 2 may in fact have bought under shared ownership, or may be referring to rent of, say, a garage or allotment).

Purchase prices and discounts

153. The homes purchased by the new buyers had a wide range of values: a quarter (26%) were valued at under £20,000, a further quarter (26%) at £20,000 but less than £30,000, and the remainder (47%) at £30,000 or more. The mean valuation was £30,430. However the effect of the discount offered under RTB is evident in that the mean purchase price (after discount) was just £14,825. 39% had qualified for discounts of up to 40%, a further 29% had discounts of 41%-50%, and the remaining 33% had discounts of over 50%. The average discount obtained was 45%, no change from the average found amongst buyers in 1986 (44%).

Sources of finance

154. Four out of five of the new buyers (80%) had to borrow money to help purchase their home. Amongst those who borrowed, the mean amount borrowed was £15,034, so overall the mean amount borrowed was £12,101.

155. In nearly half the cases where money was borrowed it was to be paid back over 25 years. A further third of loans were to be paid back over 20 years, and the remainder were for shorter periods. The mean repayment period was 21 years.

156. Building society loans were by far the most common source of finance—they accounted for 4 out of 5 of the loans received by new buyers, and overall two thirds of new buyers had one. Small numbers of new buyers had loans from banks, local authorities, insurance companies, or private sources. This appears to represent a substantial drop in the proportion of RTB purchasers borrowing money who got a loan from their local authority, from nearly half of those who bought before 1986 (43%), to less than 1 in 13 of more recent buyers (7%). The majority of buyers with a mortgage (83%) had a tax relief mortgage as opposed

to an option mortgage.

157. Nearly 1 in 10 new buyers (9%) had contributed personal savings to purchase their home, a slight drop on the 1986 figure of 15%. Small numbers had used redundancy payments (2%), money from the sale of another property (2%), or money from somewhere else (6%).

158. A quarter (24%) of new buyers had taken out an additional loan since purchasing their home. Nearly all of these were to finance alterations or improvements to the home, the remainder being for repairs. The mean amount borrowed for additional loans was just over £5,000. Two thirds of these additional loans were obtained from building societies, 1 in 5 from banks, and small numbers from insurance companies and private sources.

Worries and Difficulties

159. Nearly 1 in 5 of the new buyers (18%) had experienced problems in keeping up payments since purchasing their home. These problems related to mortgage repayments, repair and maintenance costs, rates payments, and payments of general household bills.

160. A small number (5%) had experienced problems with changing to a monthly budget, and small numbers had experienced other problems or worries since buying their home. Of these other problems or worries, only three were directly related to RTB: budgeting problems caused by variations in income; the council not doing maintenance work because the tenant had applied to buy; and one case where a purchaser reported having to refund the discount to the local authority, due to having to re-mortgage the property.

References

Central Statistical Office (1990). Family Expenditure Survey 1988. London: HMSO.

Central Institute of Public Finance and Accountancy (1989). Spring Survey of rent and housing benefits in England and Wales.

Department of the Environment (1988). Housing Trailers to the 1981 and 1984 Labour Force Surveys. London: HMSO.

HMSO (1988). CSO Monthly Digest of Statistics No. 513, September 1988. London: HMSO.

HMSO (1989). CSO Monthly Digest of Statistics No. 523, July 1989. London: HMSO.

Kerr, M. (1988). The Right to Buy: A national survey of tenants and buyers of council homes. London: HMSO.

Lynn, P. (1990). The Right to Buy: A national follow-up survey of tenants of council homes in England. Methodological Report. London: SCPR.

OPCS (1989). General Household Survey 1987. London: HMSO.

Prescott-Clarke, P. and Morrissey, C. (1988). Right to Buy: A survey of buyers and non-buyers of council homes. Methodological Report. London: SCPR.

Appendix A

Department of the Environment
Room N7/07
2 Marsham Street London SW1P 3EB

Telex 22221 Direct Line 01-276 3251
Switchboard 01-276 3000
GTN 276

Our Ref P.1062
May 1989

Dear Occupier

SURVEY OF COUNCIL TENANTS AND HOME OWNERS

I am writing to ask for your help with a housing survey which is being carried out for the Department of the Environment by Social and Community Planning Research (SCPR), an independent research institute.

Three years ago we carried out a similar survey to find out about peoples' views on renting or buying their home from the council and the results were published*. Now we are approaching residents at the same addresses to find out your views about your housing and to see whether there have been any changes in attitudes to renting or buying. You personally may have been interviewed for the last survey and if so we would very much like you to take part again. If you have moved here since the last survey we would like you to take part this time.

We would like to get your views whether you are a tenant or an owner and whether you were here three years ago or have moved in that period. Only if everyone approached takes part can we be sure of getting a full picture.

Any information you give will be treated as strictly confidential by the Department and by SCPR, and will not be passed to the council or any other organisation. The results of the survey will be summarised so that no one person's views or household details can be identified. Your address was originally randomly selected from Local Authority records. The council has been informed that this second survey is taking place but only SCPR will know who is being approached.

SCPR's interviewer carries an identification card which will be shown to you. Your participation is, of course, entirely voluntary but we would be very grateful if you could spare the time to talk to the interviewer.

If there is anything you would like to ask about the study, please contact me at the Department by telephoning me (in London) on 01 276 3251 or by writing to me at the address above. If you prefer, you may contact the researcher in charge of the project at SCPR, Peter Lynn on 01 250 1866.

Yours faithfully

Keith Kirby

KEITH KIRBY
Social Research Division

* For the results of the last survey see the book entitled "The Right To Buy" by Marion Kerr, published by Her Majesty's Stationery Office, HMSO, ISBN 0 11 752132 9, price £6.95.

Appendix B: Multivariate Analysis to discriminate between tenants and new buyers.

Form of Analysis

An investigation was undertaken of the factors which determine whether or not a household had become a 'new buyer' (i.e. had purchased their home since the earlier survey). The substantive findings are discussed in chapter 2 of the report. This appendix documents the technical aspects of the analysis undertaken.

The form of analysis undertaken was a logistic regression. This takes the form:
$\ln [p/(1-p)] = A + B X$

where p is the proportion of interests, X is a vector of explanatory variables and A and B are the parameters to be fitted.

In this case the proportion of interest is the proportion of properties that had been bought since the earlier survey (the base being all proporties that were council tenancies at the time of the earlier survey), so p can be though of as the *probability* of a property having been bought and $p/(1-p)$ as the *odds* of a property having been bought.

The vector X of explanatory variables was derived progressively, by adding factors into the model one at a time, and rejecting them if they did not make a significant contribution to the model. Significance was assessed by the standard chi-square of the difference of scaled deviances, in conjunction with assessment of the standard errors of parameter estimates. A total of 38 different variables were assessed. Each variable was initially added in to the model as an n-way factor, where n is the highest number of meaningful levels that could be ascribed to the variable. The one exception to this was the variable 'age of head-of-household' which was initially tested as an 8-way factor: more levels would have been possible, but would have been unlikely to be useful. The other 37 variables were all categorical by nature, with n varying from 2 to 7. For any variable which appeared to be significant, levels which did not have significantly different parameter estimates were combined where this was meaningful, and where effects remained significant.

The modelling was carried out using release 3·77 of GLIM, the Generalised Linear Interactive Modelling system developed by the GLIM working party of the Royal Statistical Society.

The Final Model

The final model obtained contained just two explanatory variables, each a dichotomy. These were household income, and property type. The model, and parameter estimates are shown below. The numbers in parentheses are the standard errors of the parameter estimates.

$$\ln [p/(1-p)] = A + B_{1,i} + B_{2,i} + e_i$$

where A = 2·55 (0·20)
B_1 = 1·57 (0·25) if gross weekly household income is £155 or more
0 otherwise
B_2 = −1·52 (0·39) if property is a flat or maisonette
0 if property is a house

Appendix C: Multivariate Analysis to determine characteristics of households that were more likely than others to think that certain changes might influence them to buy their home.

Form of Analysis

The analysis was concerned with the battery of seven questions asking tenants whether they might consider buying their homes if certain hypothetical changes took place. The findings from these questions are reported in chapter 3, paragraphs 78 to 96. Bivariate analysis had indicated that certain household attributes were associated with an increased propensity to think that the hypothetical changes might have an effect. The aim of the multivariate analysis was to ascertain if there were certain characteristics which described households who, across all of the seven items, were more likely than others to say the change might have an effect, and, if so, to quantify those characteristics.

The analysis used was a logistic regression, as described in Appendix B. Initially, respondent households were split into two subgroups, and each analysed separately. The subgroups were those who had said yes, and those who had said no, to the question, "Do you think you will ever buy this house/flat?" The reason for analysing separately was that the questions asked subsequently were slightly different for the two subgroups. Both were presented with the same seven scenarios, but those who thought they *would* one day buy their home were asked whether the change would influence them to *start* the buying process, whereas those who did *not* think that they would buy their home were asked whether the change would make them likely to *consider* buying their home.

Analysis of those who thought they would, one day, buy their home, revealed no variables (of the five tested) that were able to discriminate significantly between those who said that the change would influence them to start the buying process, and those who said that it would not. This was mainly because there was very little variation in the data (i.e. nearly all respondents thought the change *would* influence them to start the buying process), but also partly due to small bases. It was thus not thought appropriate to combine the two subsets of respondents for analysis purposes, as the questions obviously had different meanings in each case, and had produced very different response patterns.

Thus, analysis was subsequently confined to those who did not think they would ever buy their current home. Logistic regression was carried out, as described in Appendix B, where p was the proportion of respondents who said that, if the change took place, they *would* then be likely to consider buying their home.

Again, X was derived progressively by a forwards stepwise procedure, but only 5 variables were considered: household composition, household income, age of head-of-household, sex of head-of-household, and property type.

The Final Model

The conclusion was that most of the variation could be explained by differences in household composition (as a 2-level factor), property type (2-level), and age of head-of-household (4-level), although differences in household composition were barely significant for some of the seven hypothetical changes (the other two variables appeared significant for all seven).

A typical model is that derived from analysis of item i) in the battery—an improvement in the household's financial situation. This model is shown below. The numbers in parentheses are the standard errors of parameter estimates.

$$\ln [p/(1-p)] = A + B_{1,i} + B_{2,i} + B_{3,i} + e_i$$

Where A	=	1.16 (0.28)	
B_1	=	0.53 (0.23)	if household consists of 2 adults, no children
		0	otherwise
B_2	=	−1.18 (0.24)	if property is a flat or maisonette
		0	if property is a house
B_3	=	0	if head-of-household aged under 35
		0.79 (0.41)	if head-of-household aged 35-44
		0.83 (0.33)	if head-of-household aged 45-64
		0.13 (0.33)	if head-of-household aged 65 or over

Printed in the UK by HMSO.
821612 Dd 0293095 C19 5/91 PP.